A Girl's Best Friend

Stepping Out with the Dogs We Love

artwork by
Susie Muise

HARVEST HOUSE PUBLISHERS

EUGENE, OREGON

A Girl's Best Friend

Text Copyright © 2006 by Harvest House Publishers
Eugene, Oregon 97402

ISBN-13: 978-0-7369-1631-8
ISBN-10: 0-7369-1631-8

Design and production by Garborg Design Works, Minneapolis, Minnesota

Harvest House Publishers has made every effort to trace the ownership of all poems and quotes. In the event of a question arising from the use of a poem or quote, we regret any error made and will be pleased to make the necessary correction in future editions of this book.

Printed in China

06 07 08 09 10 11 12 / L P / 10 9 8 7 6 5 4 3 2 1

Thorns may hurt you, men desert you, sunlight turn to fog;
But you're never friendless ever, if you have a dog.

Douglas Mallock

There were ten of them—spaniels, Yorkshires, black and tans—a very regiment of tiny dogs. Often in my daydreams I think of them, and then the oppressive quiet is broken by the muffled pattering of little feet coming swiftly across the thickly carpeted floor, and my pets swarm about me, leaping into my lap, climbing on my shoulders, and frantically caressing my hands, my wrists, my cheeks, with eager little pink tongues...

The combined weight of all ten of these tiny darlings, indeed, would have come well under eight pounds. But if their bodies were small, their hearts were big. They were loyal little companions, these pets of twenty years; and as I think of the many miles along life's highway that they pattered at my side, making brighter the hours by graceful prank and unfailing love, I breathe a sigh in memory of my dogs, who were my faithful little friends.

Clara Morris
"My Dogs"
The Ladies' Home Journal, September 1902

No animal should ever jump up on the dining-room furniture unless absolutely certain that he can hold his own in the conversation.
Fran Lebowitz

There is no
psychiatrist in
the world like a
puppy licking
your face.
Ben Williams

Whoever said you can't buy happiness forgot little puppies.
Gene Hill

You ask of my companions. Hills, sir, and the sundown, and a
dog as large as myself that my father bought me. They are better
than human beings, because they know but do not tell.

Emily Dickinson

Don't you remember when, your mother laughingly dissenting, your father said that you might have him, and with rapture in your heart and a broad smile on your face you went dancing through the town to get him?

There was quite a family of them—the old mother dog and her four children. Of the puppies it was hard to tell which was the best; that is, hard for the disinterested observer. As for yourself, in the very incipiency of your hesitation something about one of the doggies appealed to you. Your eyes and hand wandered to the others but invariably came back to him.

With the mother anxiously yet proudly looking on, you picked him up in your glad young arms, and he cuddled and squirmed and licked your face; and in an instant the subtle bonds of chumship were sealed forever.

Edwin L. Sabin
"Chums"
Century Magazine, 1903

No one appreciates
the very special
genius of your
conversation as
the dog does.

Christopher Morley

I saw my little Pelléas sitting at the foot of my writing-table, his tail
carefully folded under his paws; his head a little on one side, the
better to question me; at once attentive and tranquil, as a saint
should be in the presence of God. He was happy with the happiness
which we, perhaps, shall never know, since it sprang from the smile
and the approval of a life incomparably higher than his own.

Maurice Maeterlinck
"Our Friend, the Dog"
Century Magazine, 1904

Susie Muise Studio

party

December

NYC
NYC

DOG

Susie Muise

11

The great pleasure of a dog is that you may make a
fool of yourself with him and not only will he not
scold you, but he will make a fool of himself too.

Samuel Butler

If you don't own a dog, at least one, there is not necessarily anything wrong with you, but there may be something wrong with your life.

Roger Caras

T he old theory that animals have only instinct, not reason, to guide them, is knocked endways by the dog. A dog can reason as well as a human being on some subjects, and better on others, and the best reasoning dog of all is the sheep-dog. The sheep-dog is a professional artist with a pride in his business. Watch any drover's dogs bringing sheep into the yards. How thoroughly they feel their responsibility, and how very annoyed they get if a stray dog with no occupation wants them to stop and fool about! They snap at him and hurry off, as much as to say: "You go about your idleness. Don't you see this is my busy day?"

Andrew Barton Paterson
The Dog

Polly put her hand in his, and received a hearty shake; and then she sprang over the big stove, dish-cloth and all, and just flung her arms around the dog's neck.

"Oh, you splendid fellow, you!" said she. "Don't you know we all think you're as good as gold?"

The dog submitted to the astonishing proceeding as if he liked it, while Jasper, delighted with Polly's appreciation, beamed down on them, and struck up friendship with her on the instant.

Margaret Sidney
Five Little Peppers and How They Grew

Our dogs, like our shoes, are comfortable. They might be a bit out of shape and a little worn around the edges, but they fit well.

Bonnie Wilcox

15

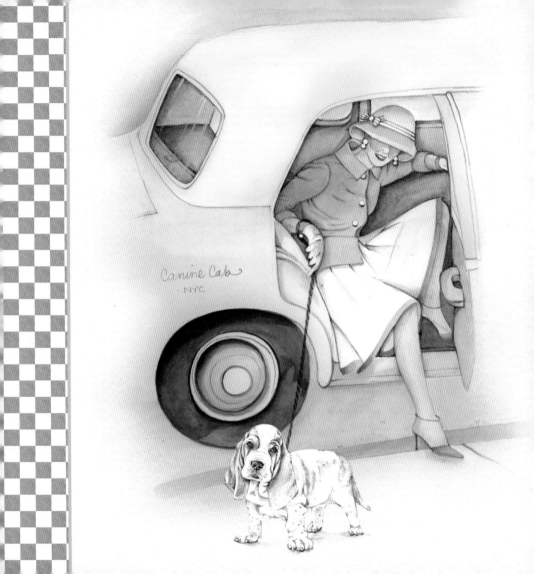

Canine Cab
· NYC

Children and dogs are as necessary to the welfare of the country as Wall Street and the railroads.

Harry S. Truman

A dog can express more with his tail in minutes than his owner can express with his tongue in hours.

Author Unknown

Toward morning, the four little hares seemed to understand that Wallie was their protector, for they came to where he had settled himself down on the floor of their home, with his nose on its doorsill, and curled themselves up against his warm body with its furry coat. So they were found when the Doctor went on his early morning round. Wallie was faithful to the guardian task he had assumed.

A.J. Robertson
"A Dog's Devotion"
The Ladie's Home Journal, September 1905

Dachshunds are ideal dogs for small children, as they are already stretched and pulled to such a length that a child cannot do much harm one way or another.

Robert Benchley

"Darling doggy, where have you been so long?" she cried, the great thing sprawling across her lap, as if he could not get near enough to his brave little protector.

Louisa May Alcott
Under the Lilacs

A dog, to be a real source of pleasure to a household, should have one master from whom it takes its orders, and naturally looks up to as its ideal. With such a bond of sympathy established between owner and dog, the latter understands intuitively whether it is pleasing its master or not; and if the dog is a companion in the full sense of the word, physical punishment, with even a fairly intelligent specimen, is rarely needed. The dog should have the consideration at its owner's hands which its loyalty and devotion merit, but should always be held to the position of a willing, obedient servant.

Adele W. Lee
"The Care of the Dog"
Outing, June 1901

hungry

thirsty

I think we are drawn to dogs because they are the uninhibited creatures we might be if we weren't certain we knew better. They fight for honor at the first challenge, make love with no moral restraint, and they do not for all their marvelous instincts appear to know about death. Being such wonderfully uncomplicated beings, they need us to do their worrying.

George Bird Evans

Dogs are not our whole life, but they make our lives whole.

Roger Caras

My little dog—a heartbeat at my feet.

Edith Wharton

One reason a dog is such a comfort: When you are downcast, he doesn't ask to know why.

Author Unknown

My goal in life is to be as good of a person as my dog already thinks I am.

Author Unknown

No matter how little money and how few possessions you own, having a dog makes you rich.

Louis Sabin

LIFE IS A BALL

I love my dog, Sarah, because she always listens to me and never talks back!

Sally Ann Schindler

Dogs laugh,
but they laugh
with their tails.

Max Eastman

I talk to him when I'm lonesome like;
and I'm sure he understands.
When he looks at me so attentively,
and gently licks my hands;
Then he rubs his nose on my tailored clothes,
but I never say naught thereat.
For the good Lord knows I can buy more clothes,
but never a friend like that.

W. Dayton Wedgefarth

An earthly dog of the carriage breed;

Who, having failed of the modern speed,

Now asked asylum and I was stirred

To be the one so dog-preferred.

Robert Frost

Blessed is the person who has earned the love of an old dog.

Sydney Jeanne Seward

The fact remains that he is there in our houses, as ancient, as rightly placed, as perfectly adapted to our habits as though he had appeared on this earth, such as he now is, at the same time as ourselves. We have not to gain his confidence or his friendship: he is born our friend; while his eyes are still closed, already he believes in us; even before his birth, he has given himself to man. But the word "friend" does not exactly depict his affectionate worship. He loves us and reveres us as though we had drawn him out of nothing. He is, before all, our creature full of gratitude, and more devoted than the apple of our eye.

Maurice Maeterlinck
"Our Friend, the Dog"
Century Magazine, 1904

27

There is no faith which has never yet been broken, except that of a truly faithful dog.

Konrad Z. Lorenz

Histories are more
full of the examples
of the fidelity of dogs
than of friends.

Alexander Pope

But as the door shut behind her she felt so left out in the cold, that her eyes filled, and when Nep, Tom's great Newfoundland, came blundering after her, she stopped and hugged his shaggy head, saying softly, as she looked into the brown, benevolent eyes, full of almost human sympathy: "Now, go back, old dear, you mustn't follow me. Oh, Nep, it's so hard to put love away when you want it very much and it isn't right to take it." A foolish little speech to make to a dog, but you see Polly was only a tender-hearted girl, trying to do her duty.

Louisa May Alcott
An Old-Fashioned Girl

Did you ever walk into a room and forget why you walked in? I think that is how dogs spend their lives.

Sue Murphy

I can't think of anything that brings me closer to tears than when my old dog—completely exhausted after a hard day in the field—limps away from her nice spot in front of the fire and comes over to where I'm sitting and puts her head in my lap, a paw over my knee, and closes her eyes and goes back to sleep. I don't know what I've done to deserve that kind of friend.

Gene Hill

I think dogs are the most amazing creatures; they give unconditional love. For me they are the role model for being alive.

Gilda Radner

Chic
Bowtique
for dogs

I once decided not to date a guy because he wasn't excited to meet my dog. I mean, this was like not wanting to meet my mother.

Bonnie Schacter

I know that dogs are pack animals, but it's difficult to imagine a pack of standard poodles . . . and if there was such a thing as a pack of standard poodles, where would they rove to? Bloomingdale's?

Yvonne Clifford

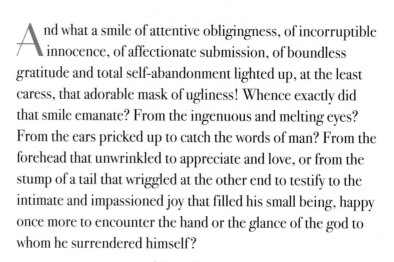

And what a smile of attentive obligingness, of incorruptible
innocence, of affectionate submission, of boundless
gratitude and total self-abandonment lighted up, at the least
caress, that adorable mask of ugliness! Whence exactly did
that smile emanate? From the ingenuous and melting eyes?
From the ears pricked up to catch the words of man? From the
forehead that unwrinkled to appreciate and love, or from the
stump of a tail that wriggled at the other end to testify to the
intimate and impassioned joy that filled his small being, happy
once more to encounter the hand or the glance of the god to
whom he surrendered himself?

Maurice Maeterlinck
"Our Friend, the Dog"
Century Magazine, 1904

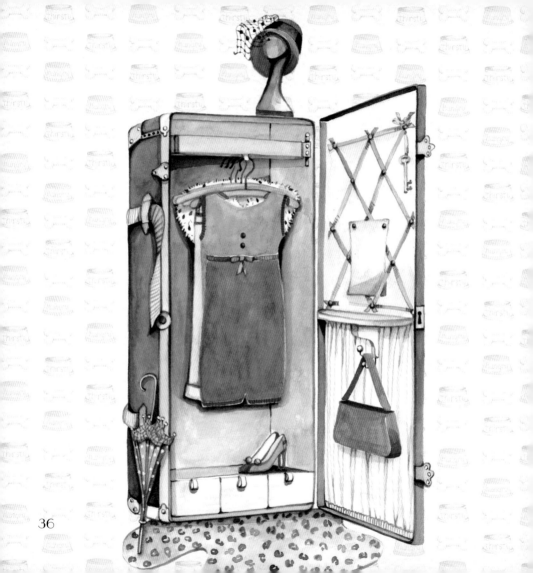

A Dog's Soul

Every dog must have a soul
Somewhere deep inside
Where all his hurts and grievances
Are buried with his pride.
Where he decides the good and bad,
The wrong way from the right,
And where his judgment carefully
Is hidden from our sight.
A dog must have a secret place
Where every thought abides,
A sort of close acquaintance that
He trusts in and confides.
And when accused unjustly for
Himself, he cannot speak,
Rebuked, he finds within his soul
The comfort he must seek.
He'll love, though he is unloved,
And he'll serve though badly used,
And one kind word will wipe away
The times when he's abused.
Although his heart may break in two
His love will still be whole,
Because God gave to every dog
An understanding soul!

Author Unknown

The servants in our house were all kind to me and were fond of me, and so, as you see, mine was a pleasant life. There could not be a happier dog than I was, nor a gratefuler one. I will say this for myself, for it is only the truth: I tried in all ways to do well and right, and honor my mother's memory and her teachings, and earn the happiness that had come to me, as best I could.

By and by came my little puppy, and then my cup was full, my happiness was perfect. It was the dearest little waddling thing, and so smooth and soft and velvety, and had such cunning little awkward paws, and such affectionate eyes, and such a sweet and innocent face; and it made me so proud to see how the children and their mother adored it, and fondled it, and exclaimed over every little wonderful thing it did.

Mark Twain
A Dog's Tale

There's facts about dogs, and then there's opinions about them.
The dogs have the facts, and the humans have the opinions.
If you want the facts about the dog, always get them straight from
the dog. If you want opinions, get them from humans.

J. Allen Boone

I wonder if other
dogs think poodles
are members of a
weird religious cult.

Rita Rudner

Give a pup a home and a little love
and he will give you his heart forever.

Pam Brown

And I'll bake a cake for Splash!" exclaimed Sue. "He likes cake. We might give the party for him," she went on. "That would be fun!"

"And they could all bring our dog presents—bones and things like that," laughed Bunny.

And so it was decided. The party would be for Splash, though of course he would not be allowed to eat all the good things. Bunny Brown and his sister Sue wanted those for themselves and their playmates.

The next day Bunny and Sue went around to the different houses, where their little friends lived, and each one was asked to come to the party. "Oh, I'm so glad you asked me!" cried Sadie West, when Sue told about the fun they would have.

"I want you more than anyone,"
was Sue's reply.

"And how funny to have the party for
Splash!" Sadie went on.

"Well, dogs like nice things."

"Of course they do. I think it's just fine!" and
Sadie clapped her hands. "I'll tie a little pink ribbon
on the bone I bring your dog."

Helen Newton said she would bring Splash a dog-biscuit.

"You buy them in a store," she said. "Papa buys them for our dog,
and you can get puppy cakes, too. Only of course Splash is too big for a
puppy cake."

"You could bring him a lot of little puppy cakes, and they would be
the same as one big dog-biscuit, maybe," said Sue.

"No, I'll bring him a regular cake, and I'll put a blue ribbon on it,"
decided Helen, and then the little girls laughed to think what fun they
would have at the party.

Laura Lee Hope
Bunny Brown and His Sister Sue

When the Man waked up he said,
"What is Wild Dog doing here?"
And the Woman said,
"His name is not Wild Dog anymore,
but the First Friend,
because he will be our friend
for always and always and always."

Rudyard Kipling

We long for an affection altogether ignorant of our faults. Heaven has accorded this to us in the uncritical canine attachment.

George Eliot

He is your friend, your
partner, your defender,
your dog. You are his
life, his love, his leader.
He will be yours, faithful
and true, to the last beat
of his heart. You owe it
to him to be worthy of
such devotion.

Author Unknown

A dog is the only thing on earth that loves you more than he loves himself.

Josh Billings